BBC MUSIC GUIDES E. B. Segel

BEETHOVEN STRING QUARTETS I

BBC MUSIC GUIDES

Beethoven String Quartets 1

BASIL LAM

UNIVERSITY OF WASHINGTON PRESS
SEATTLE

Contents

First published 1975 by the British Broadcasting Corporation
Copyright © Basil Lam 1975
University of Washington Press edition first published 1975
Library of Congress Catalog Card Number 75-5008
ISBN 0-295-95423-x
Printed in England

Introduction

When the fifteen-year-old Beethoven made his first attempts at full-scale composition he chose the piano quartet as his medium. A year earlier he had tried his hand at a concerto, but this exists only in short score and there is no record of any performance, so it may well have remained uncompleted. The second movement of the First Piano Quartet begins with a theme first noted down in C minor with the heading 'Presto sinfonia'. Evidently the boy composer had thought of writing a symphony. Unlike the string quartet, the piano quartet was a field open to youthful genius, with no precedent more intimidating than the agreeable works of Schobert or J. C. Bach. Of Mozart's two masterpieces, K.493 was not yet written and K.478 belongs to 1785, the very year of Beethoven's autograph score of his 'Trois quatuors pur [*sic*] clave(c)in, violino, viola e basso'. It was a discouraging time for a young composer who hoped to become something more than a mere epigone of Haydn and Mozart, who between them had produced masterpieces in virtually all kinds of music – symphony, concerto, opera, Mass and, of course, string quartet.

From the moment Beethoven began to publish his compositions he seems to have set out boldly to challenge the dead Mozart rather than his own teacher Haydn. The string trio Op. 3, and the piano quintet with wind Op. 16, fine though they are, tactlessly provoke comparison with Mozart's two great works in the same key (K.563, K.452); but Beethoven was notably cautious in his approach to the two kinds in which Haydn especially excelled, and neither symphony nor quartet appeared until the younger composer had established himself in Vienna with sonatas, two piano concertos (Mozart's field again), and the Septet.

Why Beethoven should have written four string trios before attempting a quartet remains unexplained. The trio medium would strike most composers as the more exacting, but there is no mistaking the complete technical maturity of Op. 3, published in 1796, four years before Beethoven wrote to his friend Amenda, 'I have only just learned to write quartets properly'.

The masterpiece that obviously provided a model for Op. 3 was Mozart's Divertimento K.563, written in 1788 and published in 1792. It was the first major work in the medium, though Haydn had written numerous small trios with two violins, and arrangements of his piano sonatas for violin, viola and cello seem to have been popular in the last years of the eighteenth century. Nothing in Beethoven's trio quite equals the great first and second movements of Mozart's work, but the excellence of the writing shows that he was already, in his early twenties, a master surpassed only by his two mighty predecessors. He uses every possibility of varying the textures, sometimes writing extended passages for two of the instruments, and scarcely ever resorting to accompaniment formulae. One might imagine that the trio was a familiar and long-established medium; Beethoven's technical command of his resources was no less wonderful than his invention.

The opening of Op. 3 combines two 'Mozartian' formulae, but their development is highly original, both being apt for unexpected key-changes. Beethoven follows Mozart closely by writing two slow movements, one in B flat, one in A flat, but he puts the serious one after the first minuet, thus making a more contrasted sequence. The minuet, very brief, is an epigram of brilliant wit, outlining a perfectly normal phrase-rhythm with silent first beats which the listener must supply for himself. After the gravely beautiful *Adagio* (a companion piece to the A flat slow movements of the piano sonatas Op. 10 no. 1 and Op. 13) the second minuet is fluent, with scarcely a moment of silence. Nothing could be more unexpected than its trio, with the wild violin solo high above the sustained chords of viola and cello. Its gipsy-fiddler atmosphere belongs to the world of Haydn, as does the neat theme of the finale. The delightful transition looks far ahead to the finale of another E flat work, the string quartet Op. 127. Evidently Op. 3 made a great impression; a piano transcription, possibly by Beethoven himself, was published in Vienna as late as 1814–15, though it may have been made much earlier.

Three Trios, Op. 9

Besides Op. 3 Beethoven wrote two of his finest early works around 1795–6, the cello sonata Op. 5 no. 2 and the piano sonata Op. 7, this latter perhaps the first of his unmistakably great compositions. About the same time he began to sketch the Op. 9 trios and the Serenade Trio Op. 8, a slight work which enjoyed immense popularity and was published in arrangements ranging from chamber orchestra to voice and piano. The young composer must have learned something valuable about the taste of the Viennese from their preference for this elegant example of 'musique de société'.

TRIO NO. I IN G

The string writing in this splendid work is worthy of the invention; nothing in the Op. 18 quartets surpasses it, and the criticism that regards its composer as a novice drawing heavily on the styles of Haydn and Mozart is nullified by the existence of this trio and its companion, the even more individual C minor.

To relate his *Adagio* introduction to the main *Allegro* Beethoven develops a trifling and unobtrusive cliché with so much wit that a quotation is demanded:

Ex. 1

The movement thus quietly introduced soon develops a magnificent energy, conveyed by trio-writing fully as sonorous as most quartets, contrasting admirably with the *pp* chords of the 'second subject' in, or rather around, the dominant minor. After the double bar the transition theme is grandly combined with the first phrase of the main theme, heard in the bass. It is the former which provides the main topic of the development, which, far beyond mere promise, is the work of a major master, as is the coda with its harmonic breadth, given by the surprise move to the flat keys suggested by the second theme.

Beethoven had already used E major for the slow movement of a G major work in the piano trio Op. 1 no. 2, a bold key-relation taken up by master from pupil, it would seem, in four of Haydn's last six trios. (Ries says that Op. 1 was first performed at the end of 1793 in Haydn's presence.) This *Adagio* belongs to the quasi-operatic type, found occasionally in all the Viennese classics, in which the violin takes the place of some heroine in an *opera seria*. A brief scherzo, rather like a Haydn minuet, shows again the deftness of Beethoven's writing for the three-voiced ensemble. (He omitted from the published version a second trio section which would have made the form ABACA.)

After the comparatively undeveloped middle movements the finale – provided Beethoven's *Presto* indication is taken sensibly – makes an impression of breadth and unaggressive power. The main theme has two contrasted ideas, the first recognisably related to the finale of Mozart's piano concerto K.449 (published in 1792), the second a self-repeating two-bar scrap of tune that has remarkable consequences later on. As in the first movement, the second subject begins on the flat side of the main key, in B flat, but by the end of the splendidly spacious eight-bar phrase (it spans two octaves) we are on the orthodox D major chord. By the double bar this move B flat → D has reversed direction, and the development begins with the first subject's opening theme, in or around B flat and G minor. When the second part of the theme appears it begins to change key in long sequences, moving further and further away from G, to be brought back at least part of the way, that is to E minor, where a mysterious passage in *pp* octaves sounds quite new, though it is derived from an accompanying figure to the second part of the main theme (Ex. 2 opposite). What follows is worthy of the mature Beethoven in his finest works; again the wonderful string writing might be the result of a long tradition of trio composition.

TRIO NO 2 IN D

The D major Trio, though at first hearing less impressive than its

Ex. 2

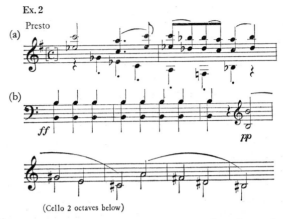

(Cello 2 octaves below)

companions, is no less the work of an original genius, at least in its first movement, in which two ideas belonging to the second subject interested Beethoven so much that he reworked them in the finale of Op. 18 no. 1. The quiet opening (note the rich tone-colour of the first phrase) uses a tonal scheme found in other 'first period' works (e.g. Symphony no. 1, the Quartet Op. 29), consisting of a restatement a tone higher in the supertonic, which here means repeating the eight-bar phrase in E minor but with a change of direction bringing it to the expected dominant. The development is full of incident, including, soon after the double-bar, a powerful inversion of the rising-scale figure of the main theme. Another stroke of genius, at the beginning of the recapitulation, is a subtle transformation that divides the theme between violin and cello, both in their highest register. The coda makes witty use of the diminished (semiquavers for quavers) form of the scale figure both up and down.

The D minor slow movement, like some of Haydn's, is not really slow at all, and its almost romantic serenade-like theme with pizzicato accompaniment belongs to the world of polite sentiment which Beethoven regarded with genial contempt. Certainly there is a touch of parody in its somewhat languishing melody.

The brief minuet could almost be by Schubert (e.g. the cadence to the first eight-bar phrase). When the mysteriously quiet trio fades into the dominant seventh chord of D the effect is prophetic of the analogous passage in the Seventh Symphony. As for the

9

expansive, broadly planned Rondo, its high cello theme over the viola's supporting bass is plainly reminiscent of Mozart's late quartet, also in D, K.575, published in 1791. Beethoven's superb sense of tone-colour may be appreciated in the horn-like octave A with which the viola supports the cello in the theme.

TRIO NO. 3 IN C MINOR

Beethoven's earliest music in C minor was the sketch for a symphony of which the theme, transposed into the very uncommon key of E flat minor, was used for one of the three piano quartets written in 1785. The sombre yet assertive mood of this theme characterises much of his first completed C minor work, the piano trio Op. 1 no. 3. Again in Op. 9 C minor is chosen for the third of the set, and again we recognise the fiery energy, the noble pathos and the lyrical contrasting theme (usually in E flat) found in all 'Beethoven in C minor'. The string trio is not, however, a tragic or even a predominantly gloomy composition. The first movement (marked *Allegro con spirito*, be it noted) is full of the heroic energy that will pervade later C minor works, e.g. the quartet Op. 18 no. 4, the Third Piano Concerto, and the violin sonata Op. 30 no. 2. The unharmonised opening phrase is the earliest version of a basic theme to which Beethoven returned at various times, notably during the years after 1820 when he was occupied with his last quartets:

Ex. 3
a) Op. 9 no. 3
Allegro con spirito

b) Op. 131
Adagio ma non troppo

c) Op. 132
Assai sostenuto

This *Allegro* is a worthy forerunner of the masterpieces of a quarter of a century later, especially in its splendid development, based on a seemingly minor detail towards the end of the exposition:

Ex. 4

After the double-bar this exchange between violin and viola becomes a single terse phrase:

Ex. 5

The return to the first subject at the recapitulation is among Beethoven's finest solutions of this crucial event in all great classical sonata movements. After an extended version of the forceful chords that had preceded the second theme in the exposition, the first four notes of the opening phrase appear, though not of course in the 'right' key, to make a pathetic sequence, so profoundly expressive that Beethoven used it, almost unchanged, in the coda of the finale of the quartet Op. 131. The four-note figure is repeated by the cello over a sustained G (the expected dominant pedal). Then, beneath the agitated semiquavers of the violin, we recognise the change of key and with it the full statement of the theme (viola and cello in octaves). At the very end of the coda the dominant passage reappears, this time over the sustained C of the cello's lowest string.

If nothing in the rest of the work quite matches this great, almost symphonic first movement, there are many felicitous touches in the elaborate *Adagio*, and the scherzo—surprisingly in 6/8 like the first *Allegro* – would hold its place in a Beethoven work of any period. It is scored with great skill, producing quasi-orchestral sonorities without ceasing for a moment to be in pure chamber-music style. The only sign of immaturity in early minor-key Beethoven – a thoroughly healthy trait in a young artist – is perhaps the explosive impatient rhetoric of such finales as those of the first piano sonata (Op. 2 no. 1 in F minor), the somewhat later Op. 10 no. 1, the quartet Op. 18 no. 4 and this C minor Trio. In the present instance this impression is dispelled by the breadth of the contrasting second theme (in E flat minor). The 'die-away' conclusion in the major key is modelled on the end of the piano trio Op. 1 no. 3.

Six Quartets, Op. 18

Whatever the cause, the marvellous certainty of technique and invention of the early works from Op. 1 to Op. 9 was slow to develop in the string quartet. Op. 18 no. 1 was sent to Beethoven's friend Carl Amenda – with a touchingly affectionate inscription on the first violin part – on 25 June 1799. Just over two years later Beethoven wrote, 'Don't let anyone see your quartet as I have greatly changed it, as only now do I know how to write quartets properly'.

Nottebohm decided on the basis of the sketchbooks that four of the Op. 18 quartets were composed in the order 3, 1, 2, 5, leaving uncertain the placing of nos. 4 and 6. Although drafts for the D major Quartet in the Grasnick I sketchbook of 1798–9 incorporate a G major theme (not used) headed 'quart. 2', Beethoven's correspondence with Amenda surely suggests that the F major, in its *earlier* version, was in fact the first: if not we would have to suppose that no. 3 was written before he had learned 'to write quartets properly'. Riemann thought the C minor (no. 4) to be the earliest of the six, attributing it on stylistic grounds to the Bonn period. A resemblance between the first movement of no. 6 and an idea in a discarded sketch of the opening scene for the Prometheus ballet, which itself comes after sketches for the Second Symphony, supports the view that it was written last of the set. The order of composition seems to have been:

I	No. 4 in C minor – probably much revised after second version of no. 1	III No. 3 in D
		IV (uncertain) No. 5 in A
		V No. 2 in G
II	No. 1 in F (first version)	VI No. 6 in B flat

Before arriving, through several stages, at the perfected form of the opening theme, Beethoven thought of his first movement as being in 4/4, not 3/4 metre. (In one of these first versions the theme was reminiscent of Haydn's Quartet in B flat, Op. 50 no. 1.) This movement takes so much of its vigour and animation from the pervasive rhythm of the theme that it is hard to believe that the common-time sketch could have gone further than the few bars attempted. Without the pulsing crotchets underneath it, Haydn's theme would have suffered from the same inability to get moving at all. With the redundant crotchet taken out of the first held note, the theme lends itself to the unison opening typical of Beethoven at all stages of his career, though his later style would scarcely have permitted, at the beginning of a sonata movement, the bold harmonies of the counter-statement. If only to counter the absurd idea, still current in some quarters, that the early Beethoven was cautiously following Haydn and Mozart, this passage demands closer comment.

Ex. 6

bars 13 ff.
[Allegro con brio]

A two-bar phrase is derived by a kind of ellipsis from bars 5–8 by omitting bars 6 and 7. By harmonising the minim as an appoggiatura, Beethoven produces the highly expressive progression used by nineteenth-century Romantics for effects of yearning and erotic deprivation. The basic chord is nothing but a diminished seventh, as may be shown by using the old notation of this type of harmony. At the third phrase (marked *x*) the tension is wound higher by a triple appoggiatura to the G minor chord on the fourth quaver. The young master who could command such resources had no need to imitate even Haydn or Mozart, and to adopt an attitude of patronage to this quartet is mere impertinence.

Having safely returned to a euphonious close in the tonic, the transition proceeds to develop the idea just described by answering the first bar over the plangent chord with the appoggiatura. This produces a splendid audacity between the upper parts (consecutive ninths *and* a false relation!); evidently a movement that can display such a range in its opening theme must have the stamina to continue as it began, and before the innocent second subject group can appear its preparation is delayed by a sudden move to A flat. The development's forceful declaration of the dominant of D minor is merely diversionary, as this closely related key has no part to play in the whole movement. What is to be developed is the first subject, beginning with a brief exchange, of Mozartian grace, on the phrase discarded after the very first eight-bar statement. The polyphonic treatment of the first bar that follows is great Beethoven of any period, and reveals the full power of the quartet medium in a way without precedent in any of the masterpieces previously given to it. This, incidentally, was one of the passages thoroughly recomposed during the revision of the quartet. The leisurely sequences over repeated quavers of the rest of the development make the happiest of contrasts, both in tone colour and in rhythm. When the recapitulation begins *fortissimo* (bars 179 ff.), the attentive listener must wonder what is to become of the expressive harmonies in bars 13–29 of the exposition. The ability both to ask such questions and to recognise how they are answered confers one of the major intellectual pleasures music can provide. Beethoven's already mature mastery guides him to leave out the whole section, which would be weakened in its effect by the powerful harmony of the development. He had already realised in the first version that this passage was too remarkable to bear repetition, but had been at some pains to make as many references to the first subject as could be crowded in. We can gain a worthwhile clue to the understanding of his methods by noting that, in the final version of the quartet, some of these thematic allusions were removed! The coda neatly combines the rising scale in crotchets at the end of the recapitulation with the ubiquitous figure

(This scale figure has already played an important role in the development, see bars 131–3.) In its harmonic range, thematic concentration and instrumental mastery, this first movement is pure Beethoven of the first order.

Amenda related how Beethoven played to him the *Adagio affettuoso ed appassionato* and asked what image it evoked. When he replied, 'The parting of two lovers', Beethoven said, 'Good; I was thinking of the scene in the burial vault in *Romeo and Juliet*'. A rejected sketch for the end of the movement headed 'les derniers soupirs' seems to confirm the truth of this anecdote. Even without such evidence, a dramatic element could be recognised in this very beautiful piece, which has an emotional expansiveness that never appears in Beethoven's purely personal slow movements.

Without overstraining the Romeo and Juliet association it is possible to find in this *Adagio* the outline of a dramatic scena in which intense feelings are expressed in dialogue, leading to a final catastrophe and collapse. At the same time everything is held within a full sonata form; the extreme violence of the coda in the minor is enhanced by the calm beauty of the second subject, recapitulated in D major. The agitated figure associated with the various climaxes is not newly invented for the purpose but is developed from a phrase in the main subject.

Schubert remembered, in the slow movement of his C major Quintet, the moving effect of this figure when given to the cello beneath broken phrases from the first subject in the development. Perhaps the coda does make excessive quasi-orchestral demands on the quartet medium, but the movement as a whole is wonderfully imagined in tone-colour (note the octave doubling of second violin and viola), and it was not until the 'Eroica' that Beethoven surpassed the tragic eloquence of this *Adagio*. Shakespeare was to write deeper plays than *Romeo and Juliet*, but *Hamlet* does not diminish the poetic truth of the earlier tragedy.

After the romantic intensity of the slow movement a minuet would be too formal, a lively scherzo too inconsequential; what follows the *Adagio* is indeed a scherzo, but one in which a chromatic element and shifting bar accents produce the kind of unrest that links it with the seriousness of the first half of the quartet. Technically it is beyond praise, the work of an absolute master of composition. Note, for instance, the resetting of the opening theme in bars 37 ff. (this was, incidentally, a *literal* repetition in the first version of the work):

Ex. 7(a)

bars 1-6

[Allegro molto]

A third harmonisation of these bars comes later (bars 64-8). It is incomprehensible that such writing should be assessed as the work of a still immature artist in process of forming his own style by imitating his great predecessors. In the third section of the four-movement sonata scheme he already surpassed them. This splendid scherzo progressively sheds its chromatic tensions in a way found in no other classic; the trio section, taking up with explosive humour a sub-figure thrown out casually in the main movement (bars 25-8) remains, at least nominally, in the tonic key and is notable for its imaginative evocation of the orchestra, which is never imitated. The concertante passages for the first violin give new significance to a device already put to admirable use by both Haydn and Mozart. Listeners who have developed long-term memory for tonal relations will enjoy the F major-D flat of the trio after the parallel juxtaposition in the first movement's recapitulation. (The same relation will recur in the finale.)

In the piano sonatas of his 'first period' Beethoven could exploit his unlimited inventiveness in exploring the resources of the instrument by writing rondo finales, a procedure continued in his concertos and reaching a culmination in the textures of the 'Waldstein'. The string quartet offered no such possibilities and demanded different solutions. The finale of Op. 18 no. 1 begins lightly with what does sound like a typical rondo theme. Listening – as we must do – without foreknowledge, we await its return in the tonic after an episode that might almost be a sonata-form second subject. This second appearance of the rondo leads to a splendidly polyphonic development, to be especially noted by critics who imagine that this composer lacked natural endowments in the matter of counterpoint. As the development begins to explore the permutations of its two themes we realise that it has endless possibilities of expansion, but after a climax it suddenly vanishes into a lyrical episode in D flat. Its subject is not new but is the inversion of a figure introduced at the close of the second subject or first episode—Ex. 8 overleaf.

Here again the first version of the quartet has, to accompany this theme, the triplet semiquavers of the main subject, but Beethoven shows how little importance he attached to 'thematic unity' by suppressing this detail in the revision. In alternation with the fugal episode already described, this melody expands with a leisurely breadth unknown in earlier works and scarcely less bold in pro-

Ex. 8

portion than the vast designs of Beethoven's middle years. Yet another stroke of constructive genius is the descending sequence of diminished sevenths at the beginning of the coda (derived from a transition figure heard earlier – cf. bars 102–8 with bars 333–45). Perhaps because it was completely composed twice over, this quartet is the most varied in expression, and the most masterly in overall design, of the six works comprising Op. 18.

OP. 18 NO. 2 IN G MAJOR

The composer of this delightful entertainment was no revolutionary. Whatever he may or may not have said to Bettina Brentano in 1810 about the deeper significance of his music, he was always ready to compose works of classical objectivity designed to give pleasure to connoisseurs. Before solitude was forced on him by growing deafness and the awful intensity of what Dr Johnson so memorably called 'the hunger of the imagination that preys upon life', Beethoven was as capable as Goethe of enjoying social intercourse and the society of active minds in all fields of thought.

The first movement of this second quartet is conventional in that the transition to the dominant is formal enough for a divertimento and the main themes are neatly contained within eight-bar phrase-lengths. However, at no time was Beethoven unwilling to find new meanings in the forms and melodic language of his earliest years; the greatest artists are not driven by feelings of inadequacy to make gestures of rejection towards the traditions that have nurtured their first beginnings.

The second group, then, is content to move in the orthodox key of D major and its relative minor; this restriction enhances the appearance, early in the development, of the main theme, now in

E flat (bar 101) and followed by a romantically mysterious passage based on the dotted phrase that follows it as at the beginning of the movement (Ex. 9). The semiquavers in the first violin part come from the second subject (bar 39), conflated with the transition in the main theme (bar 27). This wonderful passage reveals the poetic depths from which the whole delightful movement springs. (Note, by the way, the broad melodic line of the viola.)

Ex. 9

Beethoven has many ways of joining development to recapitulation – one of the crucial points in sonata style – and in this instance he takes up a seemingly casual detail from the transition. It is simply the rhythm of bars 21–2 ♩ ♩ | ♩. ♫ (for the same pattern see also Ex. 10) modified to ♩ ♩ | ♩ | which, having signalled the entry of the first subject in the cello, continues with ceremonial emphasis through the first phrase (bars 145 ff). The witty mock-heraldic effect comes from the ringing octaves of the first violin. The development had not used the first bar of the main theme, and this leaves occasion for it to develop during the recapitulation. Hence the expansion of this figure through modulating sequences, arriving at the dominant of E. Now E minor is very close to the main tonic, G major, but Beethoven chooses to give the first six bars of the theme in E *major*, with magically poetic effect. Instead of concluding in this paradoxical key, the cadence figure is repeated several times after turning back home to E minor, and the whole second group duly follows in G major. After all these highly original fresh developments a large coda is out of the question, and the movement ends with its first theme, like the Eighth Symphony more than a decade later.

Haydn, in his mature quartets, sometimes wrote slow movements as violin solo with accompaniment (e.g. Op. 64 no. 4) and the *Adagio cantabile* of Op. 18 no. 2 belongs to the tradition of the concertante movements with solo violin found in such a work as Mozart's 'Haffner' Serenade. That wit is not incompatible with its sentiment shows in the sudden transformation of the cadence figure into a rather Mendelssohnian scherzo interlude, which Elgar perhaps remembered in his Cello Concerto. The reprise of the *Adagio* extends the concertante element to the cello and finally to the whole quartet group.

The Scherzo, light as that of the piano sonata in A (Op. 2 no. 2), speaks for itself; the return after the trio section, impressive in its 'late Beethoven' spareness of texture, is most imaginatively scored: consider, for instance, the sustained open C string of the viola.

After three movements distinguished more by wit, charm and sentiment than by breadth of design, the finale, though still in the world of a comedy of manners, shows a more formidable temper – a superior version of the finale of the First Symphony. While never less than effective as quartet-writing it could, without much difficulty, be transferred to the classical orchestra. The terse theme, with its counter-statement in the relative minor, is nearer to Haydn than anything else in the six quartets, and its later developments are much in the vein of the London symphonies. Like the finale of the first quartet, this spirited piece is neither rondo nor sonata; in broad outline it is a sonata scheme with a clearly defined second subject in the dominant, later to be recapitulated in the tonic. Against this background the main theme returns several times in the manner of a rondo. Such questions of nomenclature are without importance, and we need not pursue the matter.

The second theme closes, with eighteenth-century formality, over a repeated A, the orthodox dominant, but the expected full close in D for which it prepares is evaded, leading to a deeply poetic interlude on a pedal C (the dominant of F, the key of the *Allegro* intermezzo in the slow movement). When this, still evading a full close anywhere, settles with comic insistence on the home dominant (18 bars of it!) our suspicions are aroused by such protestations of conformism, especially when this chord is in a context where it needs nothing more than a formal introduction to win acceptance. The main theme duly follows, in rondo style, but, of course, in the wrong key, for it now appears in E flat (see the first movement, Ex. 9) thus echoing the same treatment of G major and its flat sixth in Mozart's Piano Concerto K.453.

In the episode that grows out of this statement the home tonic, G, is accounted for as the dominant of C minor, but it will be some time before it is restored as the main key of the work. After returning yet again to the subdominant (C major, the key of the slow movement) the theme is reduced to its third bar, sometimes inverted:

Ex. 10

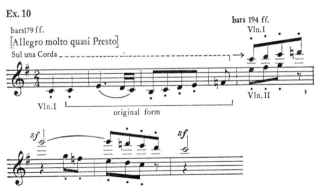

which, in a semiquaver form, has already done service in an earlier transition (see bars 112 ff.). Everything subsides for the second time on the orthodox dominant pedal, but the harmony over it is ambiguous. As soon as the ambiguity has resolved on to the long-awaited dominant chord the way is lost again. The two chords that alternate are virtually a cliché of the classical style; but whereas in Mozart the second of the pair duly yields to the first, Beethoven reverses the procedure with a pause on the 'wrong' chord:

Ex. 11

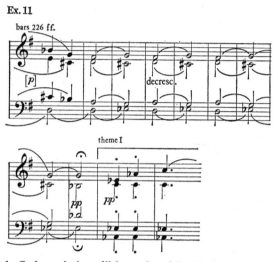

in which C sharp is inaudibly replaced by D flat so that it must resolve not back to D but forward to A flat. This is even more of a wrong key than the former E flat, and lacks confidence to maintain its identity or even to protest when C sharp reasserts itself (bars 240–1), restoring both the status quo and the main theme in G major at last. The rest of this excellent finale is given over to a recapitulation, with a brief coda in which the subdominant makes a last shy appearance, too late to gain a hearing.

OP. 18 NO. 3 IN D

Whether or not this quartet was the first of the six to be completed, the criticism that detects immaturity in it is of the kind that would complain of *Lycidas* that it lacks the grandeur of *Paradise Lost*. We shall never understand Beethoven by supposing that the exquisitely poetic opening is less characteristic than the fiery pathos of no. 4 or the *Sonate Pathétique*. Neither Haydn nor Mozart had begun a quartet quite in this way, with movement scarcely defined by the decorative violin figure over the sustained harmony of the lower parts.

The main idea of the second subject group approaches the orthodox dominant obliquely; it begins in C major, which readily turns itself into A minor. Like the first subject, this is quietly lyrical, and when the development begins with the opening theme in the tonic minor we might suppose that the whole movement is to remain in this mood. However, the development builds to a powerful climax. Classical sonata-form movements almost invariably return to the recapitulation by way of 'dominant preparation'. The development will explore key regions more or less remote from the main tonic and the logic of tonal structure demands this change of direction, back to the centre as it were – a procedure well described, though in the wrong historical context, by Browning in *A Toccata of Galuppi's*:

'Hark! the dominant's persistence, till it must be answered to.'

In the present movement the climax mentioned culminates in a chord more persistent than Browning could have imagined, but it is not the dominant (A major) but C sharp major, the dominant of F sharp minor. The chord vanishes abruptly, leaving its bass C sharp. As this drops to *pp* (do not miss the wonderful tone colour of the viola and cello at their extreme low range) the second violin places over it the two long notes of the first subject, A–G, thus turning it into the dominant seventh of D major: and the recapitulation has begun before we have had time to notice the fact. (Did Beethoven know Haydn's D major Symphony, no. 93?) At the beginning of the movement the theme had made a very Mozartian close in the tonic at bar 10, but it now takes a different course, with wonderful subdominant colour in the viola and second violin entries (bars 168–72) and the omission of the original transition to the second group. The brief coda is no less original, with its juxtaposition of the second subject (in E flat) and a final statement of the first.

The placing of the *Andante con moto* in B flat is partly prepared for by the F major and E flat appearances of the second theme in the first movement. This broadly planned rondo has something of the romantic solemnity of the *Largo* in the piano sonata Op. 7, though Beethoven is now mature enough to contrast this emotional seriousness with something more *grazioso,* a lesson from Mozart that he continued to absorb to the end of his life.

The twelve-bar theme is constructed with great subtlety; the melody, begun by the second violin, is taken over and repeated by the first before the statement has been completed. Although the general scheme is that of a rondo, the movement is unified by the highly imaginative use in varying contexts of the four-quaver figure on which the main theme is built.

The general acceptance of Lenz's division of Beethoven's work into three periods obscures at least as much as it illuminates; the third movement (*not*, be it noted, called Scherzo) could almost belong to one of the late quartets, with its undertone of pathos and its elusive rhythms. Students of music history will enjoy noting that the brief *minore* is based on the four-note figure of the seventeenth-century chaconne, used by Bach in the same key of D minor for his violin masterwork.

Though the 6/8 *Presto* finale belongs to a type not very characteristic of Beethoven, this concise sonata-form piece evidently made a strong impression on Schubert, who perhaps unconsciously echoed it in the finales of his own quartets in D minor and G major. Beethoven himself seems to have remembered its powerful polyphonic development in the Grosse Fuge, Op. 133.

OP. 18 NO. 4 IN C MINOR

The fourth quartet, though its opus number places it after the other C minor works of Beethoven's first period, shows features suggesting that Riemann was perhaps right to date it somewhere in the Bonn years. However, such a critical approach could equally well seek to place the two C minor piano sonatas, Op. 10 no. 1, and Op. 13 (*Pathétique*), earlier than the string trio Op. 9 no. 3. Perhaps a certain uneasiness in the handling of the quartet medium is caused by the absence of the piano, with its wide dynamic range and ready production of the explosive accents characteristic of 'Beethoven in C minor'. Certainly it is hard to believe that some of the writing in the first movement was the product of the composer who had already revised Op. 18 no. 1, after learning 'how to write quartets properly'.

The *fortissimo* chords of bars 13–16 and elsewhere, and the measured tremolo (in an otherwise impressive passage) near the close of the development (bars 128–35), are two instances of methods which, though anticipated by Haydn and followed readily enough by Schubert and later composers, are not really part of the true quartet style that can suggest the orchestra without such primitive adaptations of its techniques to the smaller medium. These marks of immaturity do not seriously diminish the high seriousness of this first movement. The derivation of the second subject from the first is finely imagined, especially when the second form of the theme appears in C major in the recapitulation. Such thematic relations had been made by Haydn a vital element in the evolution of classical sonata style.

Ex. 12

bars 1-8
Allegro ma non tanto

bars 33 ff.

The witty 'scherzo', less urbane than its counterpart in the First Symphony, contrasts almost too sharply with the introspective moods of the other movements. It makes a point of presenting formulae of the driest kind, but holds the listener's attention by a pervasive unexpectedness in bar-rhythms. The use of highly conventional themes gives added point to the asymmetry of phrase-lengths, for instance at the beginning, where the first four bars suggest an eight-bar phrase until the viola enters at bar 6, the first violin at bar 10, with off-beat stresses on tied notes to add further confusion for the innocent ear. When a more ingratiating 'second subject' makes a neat eight-bar phrase out of the rhythmic units of the main idea, the effect is faintly parodistic, especially in the 'old world' accompaniment and the Mozartian cadence:

Ex. 13

bars 12 ff.
[Andante scherzoso quasi Allegretto]

Only Mozart's G minor Quintet and Schubert's A minor Quartet have minuets comparable for pathetic grandeur with the wonderful third movement. If much of this quartet seems to belong to Beethoven's earliest style, the Menuetto is far beyond the criticism that seeks for influences or signs of derivation. Its first eight-bar phrase (Ex. 14 opposite) provides an example of the depth and subtlety of Beethoven's harmonic imagination. The key is, of course, C minor, but the tonic chord in the first bar seems to belong to E flat, the dominant of which is reached at the fourth bar. The harmony then moves through F minor, strengthened by its dominant on the stressed third beat of bar 5. It is only in the cadence of the whole eight-bar theme that the dominant of C minor first appears. The quite un-Mozartian chromaticism of the continuation ascends after the double-bar until the bass dwells on D flat, the 'Neapolitan' chord in C minor, though the tonic itself is scarcely present until another chromatic passage, this time descending, establishes the G major chord (the missing dominant) in the last bars. As all four movements of the work are in C the trio section, in a very diatonic A flat major, provides the sole tonal contrast. Beethoven, most unusually, directs that the repeat of the Menuetto should be played faster than the first time.

The finale, like that of the sonata Op. 10 no. 1, is abrupt rather

Ex. 14

than expansive. Like the first movement it places some strain on the natural resources of the quartet medium, which conveys agitation rather than driving energy when called upon to play rapid quaver chords. The *Prestissimo* coda displays aggression rather in the manner of the closing pages of a later quartet, the E minor of Op. 59. In the earlier work the C major of the final bars is reached by a subtle harmonic ambiguity, in that it alternates, not with its own dominant, but with the chord of F minor. To the ear, and not merely to the theorist, this suggests that C major might itself be a dominant, until the very end when the figure (Ex. 15) confirms the status of its last note:

Ex. 15

It is known that Beethoven copied out the last two movements of Mozart's A major Quartet, K.464; this supports the view that his own quartet in the same key was modelled on Mozart's. According to Czerny's reminiscences to Otto Jahn (autumn 1852), 'Beethoven once saw at my house the score of six quartets by Mozart dedicated to Haydn. He opened the fifth in A and said: "That's what I call a work! In it, Mozart was telling the world: Look what I could create if the time were right!"'

Artists develop according to their individual patterns of experience, and not in conformity with the external schemes of historicism. Beethoven's first movement is simpler, more primitive, if you like, than Mozart's; he can enjoy the straightforward formulae of harmonic transition (consider bars 11–18 and 61–5) that would have seemed too elementary for the closely woven textures of Mozart's more serious style. However, it would be an error to record such use of conventional material as a sign of immaturity. One of Beethoven's most characteristic sonatas, which he himself especially liked, is the almost contemporary Op. 22, with its rigidly 'classical' first movement. So in the A major Quartet it interests him to make a development largely out of the transition figures of the exposition, with nothing of the bold originality of the first quartet. Similarly, when the recapitulation arrives via the orthodox home dominant, it turns out to be an almost exact replica of the exposition.

Even the most literal recapitulation requires some change at the transition to bring back the second subject in the tonic, and the masters of the sonata style from Haydn to Brahms have endless resources in handling this feature of design. The cheerful unaggressive energy of this amiable first movement would be spoilt by intellectual exertions, and all that happens is that when the dominant chord arrives to announce the new theme, having been taken as a new tonic the first time, it now accepts the role of dominant, and the theme simply drops a fifth to find itself in the prescribed main tonic. Here, too, is a close parallel with Op. 22, where the same economy of device becomes a strongly individual feature of a style for which Mozart is too exquisitely sophisticated (his rusticities, unlike Beethoven's, have an air of the townsman's faint contempt for the unlettered peasant) and Haydn too impulsively inventive. Op. 22 dispenses with the coda altogether, but in this quartet it is represented by seven very formal bars echoing the beginning of the movement.

In its haunting simplicity the minuet is Mozartean, but the authentic voice of Beethoven can be recognised in the Words-worth-like plainness of speech, wonderfully characterised (when the first two-part strain is repeated by all four instruments) in the giving of the melody to the tenor voice of the viola. The trio section, unusually in the main key, has a melody very like that of the violin sonata Op. 30 no. 3, and indeed belongs to a type which appears all through Beethoven's music from the sonata Op. 10 no. 1 to Op. 110:

Ex. 16(a)

(b)

In its first form, sketched before the variations were designed, the theme of the D major slow movement suggests a verbal setting and fits Goethe's *Heidenröslein* so well that it is hard to believe it was not intended for the poem—Ex. 17a overleaf. Even this folk-song type melody was not simple enough, and in the final version (Ex. 17b) is reduced to a hexachord, A'–F♯", rising then falling to the conventional close on the dominant at the end of the first of its two eight-bar phrases. The simplicity conceals the subtle tonal plan. Binary melodies reaching the dominant at the halfway mark will normally begin a second contrasted strain in or on that

Ex. 17(a)

sketch

[Sah ein Knab' ein Röslein stehn, Röslein auf der Hei-de]

(b)

- final draft
Andante cantabile

key and return to end in the tonic. Beethoven's theme, however, begins its second half in the tonic, with a notably beautiful phrase given first to viola and cello, then repeated by the violins, with a striking contrast of tone colour. The variations, admirably diverse in textures and instrumental invention, follow the structure of the theme with a directness characteristic of Beethoven's variation style. Even when the casual ear may 'read' a variation as free, it will never distort the basic facts of the theme. Thus, in the present set, each variation has two eight-bar sections, both ending in the tonic. Halfway through, some contrasted expressive idea appears (either derived from, or corresponding to, the feature mentioned above) and the last four bars will be a recapitulation of the opening phrase. After five variations, all in the same key – note, though, the marvellously expressive reharmonisation of the theme in variation IV – it is a dramatic event when the key changes to B flat and the hexachord, now in this unexpected key, combines with its own inversion in halved note-lengths to begin the coda:

Ex. 18

This idea may have been the source of the theme itself, several years before the quartet was begun, as a sketch (in C minor) marked 'Allegretto Rondo', which Nottebohm dates 1794 or 1795, runs thus:

Ex. 19
Rondo: Allegretto

The breadth of this coda is impressive after the strictly maintained eight-bar sections of all the preceding variations.

Beethoven's finale, obviously inspired by Mozart's in K.464, is a splendid example of pure quartet-writing in which all four parts are equally important, without falling into the strict polyphony not truly characteristic of the medium. The second subject theme in long sustained notes resembles a passage in the *Pathétique* sonata, but is also related to a similar idea in Mozart's finale. For all its controlled energy, this movement is not designed for a massive ending, which would be inconsistent with the general feeling of the quartet, and the coda is perfectly contrived in its rise and fall towards the quiet final chord.

OP. 18 NO. 6 IN B FLAT MAJOR

Like the sonata in the same key, Op. 22, the sixth quartet expresses Beethoven's emancipation from the weighty influences of Haydn and Mozart in terms of a drastic simplification of the thematic idea. The main subject of the first movement is almost an alternative version of that which begins the *Allegro* of the Second Symphony. The splendid energy of this quartet *Allegro* carries the music through a broad expanse of the plainest diatonic harmony, with a counter-statement of the chord-patterned theme running straight into the no less plain transition, with its scales, up and down, and blunt statement of the most conventional key (F major here) possible for the second subject. This very simplicity both of theme and of harmonic procedures gives notable distinction to the shift of tonality to the 'flat' key area of the dominant minor. Note the glowing colour of the momentary D flat harmony in bars 57–8. It is typical of Beethoven's new harmonic architecture that the digression should be brief, and the exposition ends solidly in F major. He had by this time written a considerable number of masterly sonata movements, full of bold and unexpected turns of thematic and harmonic development. Now he can venture on something still more bold, the compelling statement of the obvious. So the development, avoiding all surprises, takes up the opening theme, still in the dominant for nine bars of the F major chord. When it moves to D major (bar 102), still with the theme, we recognise the grand breadth of 'second-period' Beethoven. After the chord, the scale; the cello begins a contrapuntal working of the transition figure from the exposition (bars 34 ff.). This lends itself to a series of fine modulations which give way abruptly to the home dominant (F major, bar 139), reached too soon, surely, to be the dominant that leads to the recapitulation in well-behaved classical sonatas. Too soon indeed, for Beethoven now shares his new-found power of expansion in a grandly deliberate progress towards this goal, delayed for thirty bars (a third of the length of the whole exposition). Like the first movement of Op. 22, this exhilarating piece attains a satisfactory conclusion without benefit of coda.

The ornate slow movement, with its divertimento-like relaxed euphony and inventive quartet-writing, plumbs no depths, though the minor-mode middle section has a reflective sobriety nearer to Haydn than to Mozart; it could evoke recollections of Milton's *Penseroso*.

We might expect as sequel one of those minuets that Beethoven continued to write long after he had moved away from the eighteenth century, but at thirty (as at all times) he still takes naïve pleasure in drastic contrasts, and the decorum of the *Adagio* is broken by the most humorously aggressive scherzo he had yet devised. Cross-rhythms, set in motion by a persistent tying-over of the last quaver in every 3/4 bar, are given a further emphasis with heavy accents so that the only way, at a first hearing, to keep track of the metre (is it 3/4 or 6/8 ?) is to count one-two-three and cling to the bass which, at least in the first section, outlines an eight-bar phrase. Normality returns with the trio, though the difficult violin solo is not conspicuous for refined taste. The blustering mock-tragic B flat minor that links trio and scherzo is especially 'Beethovenish'. The movement shows how the quartet medium makes possible a kind of texture, unplayable on the piano, that would no less surely have defeated any orchestra of the period.

Beethoven planned the introduction to the finale before he had found the theme for the movement itself. The 'Malinconia' had a clear connection with the rejected finale sketch, a relation obliterated when he arrived at the quite different theme actually used. It has often been remarked that the plan of this finale astonishingly prefigures the last quartets, especially the first movements of Op. 127 and Op. 130. In the earlier work the psychological 'programme' seems quite unambiguous. First, the long introductory *Adagio*, with its still remarkable modulations, then a cheerful (perhaps slightly facile) reaction against it; the melancholy mood recurs, but it is interrupted after only a quarter of its original statement. Attempting a further return, it is finally exorcised after two bars, and the momentary return of the *Adagio* tempo before the *Prestissimo* coda is only Haydn's familiar joke (see also the first movement of Beethoven's Fourth Symphony, again in B flat). All that prevents this admirably lucid presentation of frozen introspection yielding to healthy action from being as convincing as its composer doubtless intended is the 'alla tedesca' *Gemütlichkeit* of the main movement, not really an adequate response to the impressive 'Malinconia'. Was this strange inspiration perhaps suggested by Dürer's 'La Melancolia', so frequently reproduced and widely circulated in Germany?

Quintet, Op. 29

The Opus 18 quartets were published, in two sets, in June and October 1801. The influential *Allgemeine Musikalische Zeitung* of Leipzig described them as outstanding works ('Vortreffliche Arbeiten'), adding that they demanded first-rate and repeated performances, being hard to play and by no means popular in style. For several years Beethoven wrote no more chamber music, with the exception of the Quintet Op. 29; the very successful Septet Op. 20 was completed during 1800, perhaps while he was still working on the quartets.

Quintets with two violas first appeared in Vienna in 1773, when Michael Haydn wrote several quintets and divertimenti, followed before the year was out by the boy Mozart. Boccherini's set, only twelve against his hundred or more with two cellos, were published in 1801, a year before Beethoven's single example. Haydn had written nothing of significance in the medium, and the classics were, of course, the four late masterpieces by Mozart. Several fine, serious quintets were produced in 1802–4 by Beethoven's admired colleague E. A. Förster.

No earlier Beethoven work has such a broad, even majestic, opening as the quintet. The theme is accompanied by its own reflected image:

Ex. 20

The transition, with its formal triplet figure, is oddly reactionary after the bold innovations of Opp. 9 and 18, but when we reach the second subject the key of A minor, very close to the C major tonic, turns to the considerably more remote A major. The counterstatement turns towards F, thus restoring the disturbed tonal balance. The remainder of the exposition, like much of the development section, is dominated by the grand two-bar phrase of the main theme. Schubert-lovers will of course recognise in it the inspiration of Schubert's B flat piano sonata, a connection that becomes explicit in Beethoven's coda.

The slow movement, *Adagio molto espressivo*, is remarkable for its rich tone-colours. Without ever falling into mock-orchestral writing, Beethoven looks back to the most elevated style of the eighteenth-century divertimento (e.g. Mozart's 'Haffner' Serenade with its sublime violin solo *Andante*). Orchestral, too, in the best sense is the sonorous scherzo, another Schubertian anticipation, not least in the luxurious D flat section in the trio.

In his First Symphony, written about a year before the Quintet, Beethoven had restated his first C major theme a degree higher, in the supertonic, D minor; in both the outer movements of Op. 29 the same procedure is followed. The finale is scarcely paralleled in Beethoven's chamber music, though its strange texture of *pp* measured tremolo was doubtless remembered by Schubert when he composed his G major Quartet. The figure given to the first violin after the counter-statement explains why this piece was called 'The Storm' in German-speaking countries:

Ex. 21(a)

Op. 29 IV
Presto

(b)

Pastoral Symphony IV

The contrasting theme in triplet quavers is obviously reminiscent of the transition in the first movement, but nothing has prepared the listener for the astonishing development, where fragments of the main theme (still, of course, in 6/8) are combined with two contrasted ideas in 2/4, not for a brief episode as in the Rondo of Mozart's Oboe Quartet, but for nearly fifty bars. As its powerful climax subsides in the direction of an E major chord expectancy is tinged with bewilderment, scarcely dispelled by the unmotivated appearance of a cheerful tune in 'folk-style' *Andante con moto e scherzoso* in A major, the surprising key already used for the second subject in the opening movement. It is a violin solo arranged from an unpublished song by Beethoven himself, and the effect is of a charming inconsequentiality not common in this composer. The opening of the movement is recapitulated via F major (see the opening *Allegro* for the A major – F major connection) and all proceeds normally until there is a fresh surprise when a forceful climax in C minor suddenly turns to a pause on the major chord with G in the bass – the conventional announcement of the cadenza in a concerto. What is thus pompously introduced is the song-melody, now decorously garbed in C major. When it was in A it led to F; C is to A flat as A is to F, so on A flat the coda begins; but after all the unorthodoxies of this fantastically original finale it soon settles firmly in the home key for a peroration concerned entirely with the first subject.

The Rasumovsky Quartets, Op. 59

When Beethoven began to sketch the three works of Op. 59 towards the end of 1804, he had written the Second and Third Symphonies, the 'Kreutzer' and 'Waldstein' sonatas, and the Triple Concerto. By the time the quartets had been completed two years later he had composed another symphony, the 'Appassionata' sonata, the Fourth Piano Concerto, and perhaps above all the first version of *Fidelio* (*Leonore*). In these major works he had enlarged all the elements of composition and with them the range of experience expressible in music to such a degree that the perfection of Haydn and Mozart was no longer relevant, even as a challenge; it belonged to a different world of feeling and of thought.

OP. 59 NO. 1 IN F MAJOR

Beethoven never used a medium unless it was necessary to him, and if he could have said in the piano sonata, the concerto or the symphony what went into these three so-called Rasumovsky quartets he would not have written them.

The communicability of a musical texture depends on the co-ordination of its diverse elements. At the extremes stand the keyboard, where everything is controlled by a unit consisting of the guiding intelligence and the physical medium, and the orchestra, where the two are completely separate. The keyboard is limited by its mode of operation, the orchestra by the division of functions and the fact that the only listener in a position to grasp the total acoustic pattern is not involved in its actual physical production. Between these is the territory of the string quartet, with the expressive qualities and limitless sustaining power of the orchestra united with the direct control of the individual, not the mass.

The close study of Beethoven's themes and textures in their instrumental contexts will show that scarcely anything could be transferred from one medium to another. For instance, the first Rasumovsky quartet and the 'Archduke' trio begin with similar themes, but to interchange them would destroy both:

Ex. 22

In the trio the classic repose of the melody is present in the unemphatic quaver chords of the piano; the quartet theme, almost identical in rhythm for its first four-bar phrase, conveys at once a formidable though controlled energy, expressed in the repeated quavers typical of strings. Harmonically, this first paragraph is without precedent, and quite normal chords behave in a very unclassical way. The theme being in the bass puts the tonic chord of F into its second inversion for four bars; this 6/4 form of the triad had for several centuries been treated as a discord. When the harmony changes, half-way through bar 7, it is replaced by a strangely ambiguous form of the dominant seventh, also in an inversion, and the melody, taken up by the first violin, is frequently in almost Stravinskian conflict with it.

The spaciousness of the whole opening is evident when we realise that the first stressed tonic chord in root position arrives with the *fortissimo* at bar 19! A second theme, derived from the first, appropriately dwells on the now established F major, scored with wonderful euphony. Beethoven finds everywhere in this quartet a new way of writing for the four strings, no less spacious and majestic in sonority than the treatment of the classical orchestra in the 'Eroica'. The transition, decisively moving to C major (note the effect of the B♮, viola, bar 39), continues to develop the four crotchets of the first bar, then passes through some gloriously harsh dissonance to relax, with noble breadth, into the first melody of the second subject. To end this tonally orthodox exposition, the first theme reappears over the rich sound of the two lowest open strings of the cello.

Beethoven had at one stage intended not to repeat the exposition in the 'Eroica', but finally decided to retain it. In this quartet the opening is resumed and, within the context of the work, the first four bars must be heard as a repeat (bars 103ff.). Otherwise we lose the effect of the sudden change of direction that takes us into the development (at bar 107), so full of resource and thematic transformation that a whole essay could be devoted to it. It begins with four statements of the main theme; then, in the supertonic (G minor) of the main key, it continues with a very lightly scored dialogue on the theme's third bar with the upbeat—Ex. 23 opposite. Strange chords in minims separate this passage from the next section, a violin solo (still on the first subject) over long-held harmonies. Beethoven's power of large-scale movement enables him here to

Ex. 23(a)

(b)

bars126 ff.

achieve something new in music – an almost motionless rhythm, of wonderful breadth, through which the basic pulse is felt rather than heard. The harmony shifts gradually towards F minor and D flat, where a fresh development begins – a quiet but tensely energetic fugato on two themes, one the figure already used (*x* in Ex. 23a), the other, derived in rhythm from bars 19/20 ff. (Ex. 24 a, b and c), a variation of the first bar of the piece:

Ex. 24(a)

bars19 ff.

(b) bars185 ff.

(c)

An extended fugue would halt the unhurrying but irresistible onward movement of the piece, and soon a long descent through a diminished seventh brings the first subject, but not in the form appropriate to a recapitulation, and in the wrong key. However, everything subsides on to a dominant pedal, so this is, after all, the expected 'dominant preparation', except that what is prepared for turns out to be the second part of the theme (Ex. 24a), which, like an actor anticipating his cue, is too diffident to assert itself. Now a *fortissimo* reasserts F major as the proper key and the cello takes up the theme, its first bar hidden by the descending scale of the first violin. The classical sonata style owes much of its limitless variety in the hands of the great masters to the resource of projecting a recapitulation against the expectations aroused by a clear recollection of what has happened in the exposition. This is one reason why the full reward of the listener's experience can be won only by continual awareness of what is happening in the music without thinking ahead. Here the first twelve bars are as at the beginning, but the violin continues with a turn into the minor key (the dominant harmony is of course the same for major and minor) and within a few bars the just-established F major has vanished, so that the second part of the theme appears in D flat. The serene melody of the second subject, enhanced by a triplet accompaniment, has a new bass; everything is directed towards the final consolidation of the tonic. It is too early, though, for the end of such a grand design, and recollection of the end of the exposition produces the expectation of a further entry of the main theme. This soon appears, in full harmony for the only time in the movement.

Beethoven's symphonic codas almost invariably contain a broad alternation of tonic and dominant; and here the rising fourth of the main theme, its first note prolonged, is the material used, beginning in a close dialogue between viola and cello and rising to a climax which dies away as the first violin soars to the heights, to descend in the scale that had almost obscured the beginning of the recapitulation. Beethoven's dynamics are as functional as his structural use of theme, harmony and rhythm.

Grand though it is in breadth of design, this first movement stays within the tradition Beethoven inherited and should not have puzzled overmuch any hearer able to grasp Mozart's C major Quintet, which indeed provided an obvious model for the quartet's opening theme and proceeded to an exposition even larger than that of the later work. However, Mozart, no more inclined than Beethoven to proceed directly from a first movement of such unusual gravity to an *Adagio* or *Andante*, continues his quintet with a Menuetto of quite normal proportions. This is the Mozartean irony which works through a formal decorum to make disturbing hints of emotions threatening the stability of the whole social order within which he worked.

If, then, the first movement of Op. 59 no. 1 extends the great tradition without subverting it, the following movement is at least as revolutionary as the 'Eroica'. One of Beethoven's favourite devices in his 'middle' period was to use themes of such rhythmic distinction that their presence could be implied rather than stated, by referring to a pattern without the melody originally attached to it. In this scherzo theme he takes the extreme step of abolishing melody altogether and with it harmony, thus giving himself the utmost freedom.

Nothing can be more inhibiting to the artist than total liberty, a truth recognised by those twentieth-century composers who from Schoenberg onwards have imposed arbitrary disciplines of one kind or another on themselves in order to be able to compose at all. So Beethoven writes this scherzo (it does not bear that title) in sonata form, though the result is quite un-sonata-like in its variety of themes, key-relations and dynamics. Indeed, the classical plan is so completely hidden that the creative vitality of this wonderful piece probably communicates itself more directly to the innocent ear than to the eye of the careful analyst, noting, in the form but not in the spirit, the second subject in the dominant at bar 115 and the recapitulation beginning (with the second theme of the first group) at bar 259. The point of the sonata background is that it lends itself to continuous development and yet provides a basic ternary form when, as here, the exposition is not repeated and new ideas are introduced during the development. Even a simple analysis would identify at least seven distinct themes in this unique scherzo, the most complex and sharply contrasted of its kind. Received opinions about second-period Beethoven are based on the symphonies and concertos, the 'Waldstein' and 'Appassionata'; in all these it is reasonable to discern the simplification not only of the thematic idea but of harmonic and rhythmic device in the interests of the grand overall structure, but neither this inadequate view of

Beethoven's technical methods nor the even more *simpliste* interpretation of the content of his music as 'optimistic' can survive the experience of the Rasumovsky quartets.

We need not impute insincerity to Beethoven if we recognise in the orchestral works an element of public oratory appropriate to the medium. Hence the cumulative reiterations of small units built into large paragraphs, the expansion of formal proportions with almost empty spaces containing little but modes of vibration. All this, so far from being a defect, is characteristic of supreme mastery. A convincing if laborious demonstration of the differences between symphony and quartet would be to transfer to the orchestra the scherzo of Op. 59 no. 1. That which in the four strings is totally convincing in its alternations of wit, rough humour, lyrical calm and formidable violence would seem excessive and crude, even expressionistic, in terms of the much more extreme contrasts of the orchestral medium.

Beethoven wrote over the beginning of the slow movement words which hide rather than betray some deep personal involvement. They run 'A willow or acacia over my brother's grave'. As both Johann and Karl Beethoven were alive at the time this strange inscription has been dismissed as meaningless, but the music is elegiac, with a brooding intensity far from common in Beethoven, though there is an obvious affinity suggested, partly by the F minor tonality, with Florestan's soliloquy. (We remember that early work on these three quartets was contemporary with the first version of *Fidelio*.) This music is, of course, above autobiography, but it is perhaps allowable to find something personal to Beethoven's lost hopes of happiness in the words sung by Florestan in the aria following the F minor Introduction: 'In des Lebens Frühlingstagen ist das Glück von mir geflohn' ('Happiness has fled from me in the springtime of my life'). As for the enigmatic reference to 'my brother's grave', Ludwig was the second bearer of his name, as his parents' first child died a few days after he was born.

The main theme of this *Adagio* is unusual for Beethoven in its wide intervals, a feature of many Romantic melodies with their exploitation of emotional tension, and reaching its extreme form in the prevalent minor ninths and major sevenths of the musical Expressionists. As a rhetorical device, the equivalent of histrionic gestures expressive of grief or astonishment, these wide melodic intervals reach far back into history, but when Beethoven's themes are not triadic, conjunct motion and thirds are extraordinarily prevalent, both in *allegro*s and in slow movements. It is at the least a striking coincidence that of the three slow movements in minor keys in all the quartets, two have this rare type of melody, and both are known to have been associated in the composer's mind with images of death (see p. 15).

The later theme compresses into a single phrase no fewer than three of the devices associated with the expression of a personal type of pathos Beethoven scarcely ever permitted himself, notably the appoggiatura, the large falling interval, and the 'false relation'. Thus the very first bar of this deeply felt elegy makes an effect of 'calm despair', especially telling after the tremendous vitality of the preceding movement. Never has so much been expressed with the elementary progression of tonic and dominant chords:

Ex. 25

Before the cello takes up the theme it provides a bass of which a twice-heard figure is rhythmically identical with the austere phrase that makes up the 'second subject':

Ex. 26

The formal close of the exposition in C minor (four bars of this very slow tempo) gives great emotional force to the resumption in A flat of the theme quoted. Sudden harmonic changes would diminish the grandeur of this movement, which restates, in the more personal medium of the quartet, much of the *Marcia funebre* of the 'Eroica'. Thus the vehement climax, early in the development, on the remote chord of D major (bar 55), is reached by graduated steps and immediately explained as the dominant of G minor. Four bars stay in A flat, for the second violin repeats the two-bar phrase given to the cello. Three more bars move towards D flat (bars 50–2), but consolation is not thus easily to be gained and this flat sub-mediant is minor, not major. So is the chord that follows, and somewhere in this 'darkness made visible' there is an enharmonic change – D flat minor → G flat minor = C sharp minor → F sharp minor → D major. The openings of the 'Appassionata' and of the quartet Op. 59 no. 2, show the normal major flat supertonic, and if bars 53–4 were D flat followed by G flat (both major) the sequel would be a return to the tonic of the movement, F minor. As it is, the threatening manifestation vanishes like some Shakespearian ghost and the development continues with a wonderfully scored dialogue on the first theme, over a pizzicato bass. Noting that we must not have foreknowledge, we arrive at what is surely dominant preparation of the orthodox kind. The pizzicato figure pervades the whole texture and the viola line hovers over the open C string. All this is sheer drama, as, with the only ritardando in the piece (bar 70), the harmony shifts, the viola's C rises as movement revives, and the first violin begins a long cantilena in the consolatory D flat major expected, but withheld, in the passage described above. At its end the viola repeats (subtly changed) its C string figure (cf. bar 69 and bar 82) but this time the open C, now in staccato semiquavers, really is the home dominant and the recapitulation begins, completely rescored and condensed by the suppression of the counterstatement. The elaboration of the melody, not altogether felicitous, makes an oddly operatic effect: perhaps something of the rhetorical pathos so nobly renounced by the composer of *Leonore* found its way into this most personally expressive of *adagio*s. At the end of the recapitulation, notably exact in its cadential figures, Beethoven presumably intends some striking change of harmonic direction for the extended coda that surely is demanded by such a broadly proportioned movement. Not at all; the full close into the tonic at bars 113–14 begins a further complete statement of the main theme, as though this sonata design were a vast rondo of unpredictable size. The last bar of the melody expands so that a close in F minor is evaded and C major acquires its own dominant seventh, a procedure that gives it the solidity of a key too firmly established to allow any return to F minor. As the first violin sets out on its long cadenza in this bright major mode, the sombre mood of the *Adagio* is not so much contradicted as dispersed or blown away by the morning wind.

This is one of those transitions with which Beethoven sometimes wounds the tender susceptibilities of romantic souls. More drastic expressions of his indestructible sanity in refusing to use either contemplation or introspective gloom as an escape from the world of normal living may be found in the Violin Concerto, the C minor Symphony, the 'Archduke' trio and, transcending even these, the *Hammerklavier* sonata. In the present work, having been perhaps a quarter in love with easeful death, he builds the splendid finale, full of creative joy without taint of 'Teutonic will', on a tune steeped in Slav melancholy. We need not regard this as a misunderstanding of the aesthetics of folk music, though it is permissible to speculate about Count Rasumovsky's response to this interpretation of his patronage. The key of this quartet is F major, but the tune is indubitably in the minor. Nottebohm says that Beethoven possessed and himself annotated a copy of Ivan Prach's collection of Russian folk-tunes, in which the theme used is given in G minor, with the marking *molto andante* (!). Now, he was not under contract to adopt this particular melody, but the challenge to his resourcefulness was evidently not to be resisted, and he chose to conscript into a major key *allegro* this decidedly pensive minor-mode theme. The method was simply to double the speed and compel the tune to adapt itself to F major against its clear wish to be treated in D minor by setting its first half against a dominant pedal and refusing to allow it to close in D minor—Ex. 27 overleaf. At the first statement, as the quotation shows, it does manage a fugitive cadence in its proper key, but the counter-statement ends, or rather, fails to end, on a B flat bass. In the recapitulation this is rudely emphasised by a full bar of B flat and D (bar 319), an affront to the tune only just redeemed by the magical harmonisation bestowed on it, for once at the proper speed, in the coda. The counter-statement inverts the treble-bass combination and this,

Ex. 27

Thème Russe
Allegro

pleasing in itself by its economy, has a further consequence. The first movement had begun with a bold harmonisation of its diatonic theme in which the tonic chord appeared in its second inversion (the 6/4 chord). The shape of the 'thème russe' is such that when it is in the bass the F major chords are either in root position or first inversion. By inverting the combination (again with a persistent dominant – the trilled C) Beethoven produces 6/4 tonic chords, a rare feature in classical harmony which makes a subtle link between first movement and finale.

It is often remarked that folk-tunes resist development and can only be repeated, but Beethoven treats his Russian theme with as much resource as if it were his own invention. After the second statement another begins in the striking sonority of the deepest viola tones, but this is not completed and is absorbed in a new idea in poised descending thirds. The transition with its admirably idiomatic first violin part is, of course, based on the opening bars of the 'thème russe'. The 'second subject' shares with the first and with the first movement theme the feature of a persistent pedal, here in the high octave Gs of the first violin. It too has a counter-statement in the manner characteristic of the whole quartet (a unifying device more potent than the often imaginary relations between themes); this, in the minor key, has a tone-colour of symphonic depth, with the G pedal in octaves (violin II and viola) in the middle of the canonic dialogue, at three octaves distance, of cello and first violin. The return to C major for a further theme in the 'second subject' is delayed by a very telling reference to the beginning of the first subject, a formal device Beethoven had used as early as the piano sonata Op. 10 no. 3. The theme thus intro-duced is a tonic-and-dominant figure given great distinction by the syncopated rhythmic pattern which is to prevail, with orches-tral power, in the development. Though the reference is without formal significance, the rising scale and broken thirds that end the exposition are clearly derived from the violin's cadenza in the last bars of the *Adagio* (see bars 130–2 and 222–7).

The development begins, like the exposition, with the long trill on the dominant, and the entry of the cello (doubled this time by the viola) on the tritone (F♯-c″) is a highly accurate expression of the features in Beethoven's character that had worried Goethe, who would certainly have shown more respect for the ambassador to whom the work was dedicated.

This F sharp makes a further connection with the first move-ment. Beethoven's first opening movement which did not repeat the exposition was that of the C minor Violin Sonata, Op. 30 no. 2, and the *locus classicus* for this procedure is of course the 'Appas-sionata'. In the F major Quartet the first subject begins, at the end of the exposition, as though a repeat were intended, and it is not until the fifth bar that this expectation is firmly dismissed by the intru-sion of the note G flat. Here are the two passages for comparison:

Ex. 28(a)   bars 103 ff.

Ex. 28(b)

In this development Beethoven uses a method of thematic change found in Bach, the widening of a melodic interval without changing the rhythm, so that the phrase retains its identity. A splendid example in Bach is Contrapunctus IV in the *Kunst der Fuge,* from which Beethoven copied excerpts in one of his later sketchbooks. Bach uses it thus:

Ex. 29

The 'thème russe' of the finale has the figure of a rising third which, with admirable effect, is increased to a fifth thus:

Ex. 30

After a resonant climax on the dominant of D minor (bars 262 ff.) this becomes further extended to an octave, then to a sixth, and back to a fifth:

Ex. 31

49

The tonal scheme of the development is marvellously subtle, both in itself and in its relation to the whole movement. The passage beginning with Ex. 32 modulates away from D minor, but the second theme of the dominant group in the exposition to which it leads restores the D minor centre by treating the E flat tendency of bars 270 ff. as its flat supertonic. The closing section, one of the finest things in the work, begins in D minor (note the first subject in the viola), and though the return to the recapitulation could easily be made from this accessible region the reprise begins in, or around, B flat, an error lightly corrected in the second bar of the hard-tried Russian theme. Why the insistence on D minor? It is the key in which, as explained earlier, the theme is forbidden to make its cadence; melodically it does this, but the harmony refuses to conform, and Beethoven's unfathomably ironic humour gives us the desired tonality but without the theme. Its last appearance at the very end makes a feint of admitting the dominant of D minor, but it is too late; the melody expires before it can reach its conclusion.

The rough *Presto* is as indefensible and as characteristic as Beethoven's puns. Two details in the coda reveal the acute mind shaping all this seemingly impulsive invention. The trill on the C finally asserts itself on all four notes of the home dominant seventh (note that it is omitted in the reprise) and the four *sforzando* crotchets following this tumultuous chord are an augmentation of the sixth bar of the 'thème russe':

Ex. 32

So much for its claim to be in D minor!

The second Rasumovsky quartet begins with a movement tense rather than tragic, adapting to purposes wholly serious the contrasts of the *Allegretto vivace e sempre scherzando* second movement in the previous quartet. Clearly this wide range of expression is facilitated by the use of the mediant or 'relative major' for the second subject; besides which the flat supertonic of the opening (as in Op. 57) provides a motivation for an unprecedented range of key in the development and coda. Beethoven had discovered in the slow movement of the E flat Sonata, Op. 7, the power of silence, and in this quartet the empty bars are even weightier than those of the similar opening in the 'Appassionata'. Early sketches show that these silences were the product of Beethoven's recognition that the theme, as first conceived, needed broadening in its phrase-lengths:

Ex. 33

In the sketch E minor is inadequately stated; hence the opening tonic and dominant chords, seemingly the merest formula, which later reveal profound meaning. In fact the theme comprises, within eight bars, three distinct elements; the two chords, the silent bars, and the two-bar melodic figure.

Beethoven has no set procedures, and the only connection between this first movement and that of the previous quartet is the presence of transcendent genius. The one is spacious, with slow-moving harmonies and a counter-statement of an already extensive theme; the other immediately contradicts its main

tonality and without counter-statement begins to develop the
first figure before proceeding to state a wealth of further distinct
thematic ideas. These emerge from a polyphony that would be
notably complex in a Brahms development; it is a revolutionary
innovation in this context at the opening of an exposition. The
process is contrapuntal inversion and continuous variation. Thus
bars 21 and 22 reproduce bars 13 and 14 with the parts exchanged
so that the viola's melodic line rises to the surface. Harmonically,
the F major of the opening is too subversive of the tonic to bear
elaboration, but the idea of F natural in E minor is developed in
the implied C major of bars 16–17, the suggestion becoming solid
fact in the *fortissimo* dominant seventh of bar 26, resolving with the
utmost rhetorical grandeur on the triad not of C major but of C
minor. The direction is towards the orthodox mediant, as the
second subject is to be in G major. This involves the establishing
of its dominant, and a further splendid stroke is the E flat chord at
bar 30, reflecting the Neapolitan harmony of the first theme. When
the viola's pedal point on D has established a new key, the first
violin's initial articulate melodic phrase develops the rhythm and
outline of bars 13–14:

Ex. 34·

bars 13-14
Vln. I
bars 36-37

and the first half of this bar is of course the origin of the forceful
chords in bars 49–50 and 53–4. Again the very expressive falling
sixth of bar 48 (indeed the whole phrase) is almost quoted from the
first subject.

These allusions give a peculiar density and concentration to the
first part of the movement, a character emphasised by the elusive
tonality, with its pervasive chromatic inflections frequently
contradicted within the phrase. As the movement proceeds it
becomes clear that the relation of two triads a semitone apart,
stated in the first subject, is the 'theme' of the whole piece. For
instance, the solid G major that ends the exposition is modified
in the repeat by falling a semitone to lead into the development.
This would be impressive enough if the E flat thus introduced were
to be the key of the development, but the expectation is contra-

dicted by the shift to B minor, a process to which the silent bars give mysterious depth. The B minor, so firmly stated, is at once abandoned for the broad lyrical sequences on the first subject that seem to be no less firmly set around the remote region of A flat (or G sharp). However, Beethoven is not interested in unmotivated mystification, and the harmonies move back to B minor, though the triad of this key remains in 6/4 position (see bars 13–14 where the home tonic is treated thus). Continuing the Neapolitan relations of the first subject, B minor gives way to C major-A minor for the first great climax on the continuation of the opening chords (reduced to single notes) with the semiquavers of bar 15 in which this combination is already implicit:

Ex. 35

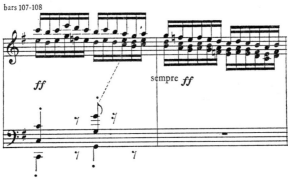

A minor is temporarily then decisively displaced by B flat, and the bass rises by semitones through the tritone to the unharmonised climax that serves the structural function of restoring the home

tonic for the recapitulation. This powerful utterance is a development of the most lyrical theme in the movement:

Ex. 36

The original silent bar is filled by semiquavers, and the first subject
group is condensed to allow room for the expansion of the second
to give due weight to the tonic major, with ironical promise of a
happy ending. Before the coda, though, E major yields abruptly
to the dominant of E flat for the repeat of the whole development
and recapitulation. When we return to this point the tonic minor
supervenes with grim decisiveness, only to turn to C major (bars
107 ff.) which, inflected to its minor, begins the sublime modulations of the coda, in the broadest harmonic motion in the movement; the dominant minor ninth (see the coda of *Leonore* No. 3)
builds up in the syncopated chord pattern that has appeared (a)
at the end of the exposition, (b) before the C major climax in the
middle of the development, and (c = a) at the end of the recapitulation. The final unison statement of the opening phrase looks
ahead to the Ninth Symphony.

I have dealt at length with this wonderful movement because
its complexity of harmonic and thematic integration makes non-
sense of the still maintained view that 'second-period' Beethoven is
characterised by elementary blocks of simple diatonic harmony, of
which the surfaces are equally simple themes.

Though the Romantics found something especially characteristic in Beethoven's *adagios*, of which the one in this quartet is
perhaps the finest, the class is small if classification excludes
variations. In all the symphonies, quartets and piano sonatas,
there are scarcely a dozen, of which half belong to the early period.
The rest are found in what may, without disrespect, be called
lesser works, including the Quintet, Op. 29, and several violin
sonatas.

Czerny (to Jahn) and Holz stated independently that Beethoven
said the idea for the slow movement came to him as he gazed at
the star-lit sky, thinking about the 'music of the spheres'. J. A.
Stumpff, who later sent Beethoven from London the complete

set of Handel's works in Arnold's edition, visited him in 1824 and wrote an account of several meetings during his stay at Baden. During a country walk, he relates, Beethoven said, 'When I contemplate . . . the host of . . . suns or earths my soul rises to the source of all creation. . . .' He is known to have read Kant, from whose *Theory of the Heavens* (1755) he may have taken these ideas, and, as is well known, was fond of the Kantian phrase about the starry heavens above and the moral law within. To quote all this is not to suggest that the music is programmatic, but to note its association with one type of the highest reach of the imagination.

Like the *Adagio* of the F major Quartet, the piece is in a full sonata form, but the normally contrasted themes and tonalities are woven into a continuous texture, the only structural feature to be emphasised being the dominant pedal before the recapitulation. The chorale-like theme materialises as from a great distance with successive entries of the four voices in both four-bar phrases, the second deepening the mystery with its initial D♮'. Note that the counter-statement (in violin II and viola octaves) is reharmonised beneath the strange rising scale of the first violin, in a rhythm that turns into the dotted figure prominent in another profound *Adagio,* that of the Fourth Symphony. Here it gently impels a theme of marvellously plain felicity. Such things in Beethoven almost persuade one to propose a musical Platonism and to suggest that he discovered rather than invented the ideal forms in which the art shows its highest conceivable perfection. Be this as it may, Heaven is not the place for chromatic harmony.

The second subject is even simpler, with the already calm dotted figure replaced by the broad tranquillity of triplet quavers. The exposition becomes almost static as it rests on a dominant pedal (bars 48–51) and passes imperceptibly into a restatement of the main theme in B major. Its second strain moves into D with a vehement climax of startling brevity, after which the 'codetta' figure of bars 48–9 broadens into slow modulations, arriving at B flat in bar 63. What follows, awe-inspiring in its intensity, is prosaically to be described as a rising sequence on the first two minims of the whole movement, leading to a climax in which the chords of F sharp minor and G major are twice heard in succession – the Neapolitan effect of the first movement. When the prolonged dominant preparation for the reprise arrives there is no place for the relaxed human warmth of its major triad, and the

dominant minor ninth of the first movement coda, now cold and
distant as starlight, haunts the listening ear until the theme enters.
The return is to the counter-statement and the melody is again
reharmonised (Beethoven shows here a Bach-like power of varying
the treatment of a chorale), with the pervasive rhythm now in the
bass, where it remains through the whole of the first subject
group. The effect is not unlike Shakespeare's

> 'There's not the smallest orb which thou behold'st
> But in his motion like an angel sings . . .'

The wonderful second melody is extended (compare especially
bars 16–18 with bars 92–4), and the modification necessary to keep
the recapitulation in E major is begun by the viola:

Ex. 37

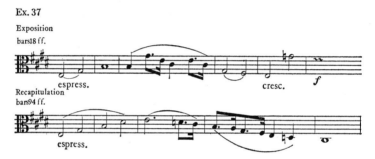

The long tonic pedal that now prevails is broken by the very
surprising return of the chorale. Beethoven was not one to heed
Johnson's warning that he who has experienced the unutterable
would do well not to attempt to utter it. As the barely realisable
vision fades, the end of the theme is almost lost in the deep register
of the viola, and the subdominant touch appropriate to a coda
comes from the inflection of the codetta figure between D natural,
C natural, C sharp and D sharp, even this vague disquiet vanishing
before the last bars.

While Beethoven was working on the first movement he noted
down sketches both for the slow movement and for an unremark-
able *Tempo di Minuetto* in E major, appropriate neither in key nor
in any other way to follow the sublime *Adagio*.

The Brahmsian *Allegretto* that soon replaced it needs little comment. Its bare textures look forward to late Beethoven, but the
troubled restless brooding of the opening, alternating with out-

bursts of undirected energy, is characteristic of the Beethoven of whom Goethe was to write (letter to Zelter, 2 September 1812), 'His talent amazed me, but unhappily his is a character utterly lacking in self-control'. Perhaps he had more to control than his august contemporary (control is never lacking in the music), but these quartets are not directed towards social occasions. It is not by chance that the *forte* is each time in F major, a further consequence of the opening theme of the first movement.

When he arrives at the 'thème russe' that serves as trio to this gloomy non-scherzando scherzo, Beethoven makes no attempt to develop his theme but repeats it, seemingly *ad infinitum* in a good-humoured parody of academic counterpoint, becoming openly derisive when, before making amends, as he had done in the finale of the first quartet, by an exquisitely sensitive harmonisation of the alien theme, he forces it into canonic imitations which refuse to 'go'. By insisting on a double repetition both of *minore* and trio section, he leaves at the end of the movement a strange sense of unresolved contradictions.

All sketches for the finale, even before the theme appears in recognisable shape, share with it the tonal feature of beginning on C major and remaining there until the cadence. To say that the finale begins *in* C is an over-simplification. Any bad composer can start a piece in the 'wrong' key; the genius here is to dwell on C while making it perfectly clear that the cadence into E minor in bars 8–9 is the real truth of the proposition. Sketches for the theme show the gradual elimination of superfluous C major elements. The function of this tonal ambiguity, apart from the cheerful demolition of classical harmony, is to connect first and last movements by reminding us that the climax in the development in the opening *Allegro* had been in C major, such a reference being one of Beethoven's methods of unifying a work. When a new theme is due it is in the dominant minor, for to use the relative major here would give inappropriate weight to C major by stressing its dominant. However, the preparation for the later returns of the main theme deliberately dwells at almost inordinate length on the figure D-E-F natural (compare this with bars 114 ff. in the finale of Op. 18 no. 3). The last page, *più presto,* expresses mock fury in its clenched-fist insistence that E minor has been the main key all the time. Exhilarating though it is in its humour and force, this finale fails to attain the level of the first and second movements.

When the three quartets appeared, critical reaction showed the hostility of incomprehension, but the third of the set was found less unacceptable than its companion works. A favourable reviewer wrote: 'The third in C major . . . cannot but appeal . . . because of its originality and melodic and harmonic force.' We have already noted Beethoven's admiration for Mozart's A major Quartet, and he could not but have been impressed by the introduction to the last of the set of six to which it belongs, the so-called 'Dissonance' Quartet in C, K.465. The Mozartian character, regressive in the Beethoven of 1806, of a discarded sketch for Op. 59 no. 3 supports the view that its mysterious slow introduction was inspired by the earlier work; and Mozart's influence, scarcely traceable in the symphonies and concertos, may be found in the whole quartet, even to virtual quotations. Ex. 38 shows two transition figures.

Beethoven's introduction, unlike Mozart's, deliberately obscures not only tonal structure but rhythm also. The direction *Andante con moto* is surely ironical, for motion is notably lacking in nearly thirty bars of 3/4 almost devoid of crotchet movement. Here is the music for Dante's image of being lost in a dark wood, unable to find the right way. The sudden emergence of C major when the long-held diminished seventh resolves (on a weak beat) is not really predictable, since this chord offers a choice of directions. As for the theme, such a prolonged lyrical melody had already opened the D major Quartet of Op. 18, but the withholding of harmonic support except for the cadence produces a kind of opening quite unlike the first subjects apparently normal to middle-period Beethoven. For the counter-statement the theme moves up a tone to the supertonic as in two earlier C major works, the First Symphony and the String Quintet. The use of the same structural device in the first movement of the 'Waldstein' sonata completes this interesting evidence of Beethoven's key associations (the origin of these C major supertonics is in the sonata Op. 2 no. 3, where the melodic figure is repeated sequentially in this way but without the change of harmony).

The upbeat figure ♪·♪ | ♩ becomes so important that it, rather than the theme it introduces, may be taken as the principal idea of the movement. Most of the actual themes are formulae clad in plain, almost subfusc harmony, as though Beethoven deliberately chose

Ex. 38

Mozart, K.465, I
bars58 ff.

Beethoven, Op. 59 no.3, I
bars61 ff.

[Allegro vivace]

to exercise his powers of mind in creating a masterly sonata movement out of what most composers would regard as 'unconsidered trifles' – something he was to do again in the Diabelli Variations. Perhaps he was conscious of the supreme demonstration of this possibility in the finale of Mozart's last symphony; his own example can bear the comparison, not least when the two-note subject makes the principal climax at the end of the development by extracting antiphony from the four strings, the overlapping phrases producing splendid harmonic audacities by the simplest means. The overlapping thirds are comparable with those in the third *Leonore* Overture.

The reprise brings the variation principle to the centre of sonata-style formal structure; in the violin theme what is recapitulated is not the melodic line itself but the idea of which the original is one realisation. Besides this the upbeat motif is elaborated with a subtlety that recalls the introduction by giving it imitative entries in the three lower voices and merging it into a trill in the first violin part. Even the blunt seventh-chords of bars 41–2 are brought under the spell of these chromatic mysteries. The whole theme, always *pianissimo*, becomes wraithlike until the return of the first transition, unchanged in its prosaic and strenuous C major. After this everything proceeds with almost the regularity of the sonata Op. 22, and the coda is the shortest in any major Beethoven work, though here too the motif is not forgotten. It is the play of a first-rate intellect with this insignificant fragment that gives to this movement a fascination more than sufficient to compensate for the only partial integration of its formula-type themes with such profoundly original inventions as the reprise.

The presence among the sketches of the theme that became the *Allegretto* of the Seventh Symphony suggests that it was intended for this quartet, but its nature, realisable in cumulative repetition, needed the orchestra, and Beethoven seems to have left it as an isolated *Einfall* and to have turned to the present movement.

This strange though wonderful invention eludes all classification and seems to belong to a world alien to ordinary experience – 'Errantes silva in magna sub luce maligna'. For more than three-quarters of its considerable extent the motion of six quavers in a bar is maintained, and the characteristic dynamic nuance is the *crescendo* frustrated by a drop to *piano*. Even the prevailing type of melody is most uncommon in Beethoven, consisting of figures that fall away from an early stress—see Ex. 39.

Those few bars epitomise the remoteness of this extraordinary piece from the norms of classical styles. Only the C major theme, introduced like a sonata second subject, contrasts, perhaps too drastically for complete conviction, with this unique expression of *accidia*, the melancholia peculiar to those who were given to prolonged solitary meditation.

A typical Beethoven scherzo would be as inappropriate a sequel

Ex. 39

here as in the E minor Quartet, and a minuet was planned from the
early sketches to the finished work, though at first in a different
key – F major with the trio in D flat. At the end of the sketches of
the final version Beethoven wrote 'Finale C moll', which suggests
that he thought of reversing the tonal scheme of the Fifth Symphony, on the plan of Haydn's Quartet in G, Op. 76 no. 1. As the
symphony was at one stage to have had a minor-key finale, perhaps
the theme sketched for this might have been considered for trans-
ference to the quartet. It shows a strong Mozartian influence,
being almost a paraphrase of the variation-theme of the finale in a
work Beethoven is known to have greatly admired, the Piano
Concerto K. 491.

Ex. 40   L'ultimo pezzo

Some years later, Beethoven wrote a quartet finale full of lofty pathos (Op. 95), but at this earlier stage of his experience he had by no means exhausted the possibilities of the heroic style, and the C major Quartet, with its Mozartian background, culminates in a finale inspired by the sonata-polyphony of the 'Jupiter' Symphony. Its *moto perpetuo* theme emerges from the minuet through strange modulations reminiscent of the introduction to the first movement. The drift of the harmony is towards C minor, and this coda may well have been designed to introduce a finale based on Ex. 40. In the event the shift to C major in the last two bars creates a moment of drama. Over a sketch for the C major theme finally adopted to complete the quartet Beethoven wrote 'Let your deafness no longer be a secret, in Art as well [as in social life]'.

Both the theme and its exposition have been criticised on the false assumption that Beethoven was attempting a fugue. There are indeed successive entries in tonic, dominant and tonic positions, but the formal argument of fugue would destroy the essential quality of this opening, with its immediate release of a stream of energy. The sense of creative force set free from doubts and brooding uncertainty is not gained through argument. As for the ten-bar theme, the attentive ear will take in, without necessarily grasping analytically, its coherent melodic structure, beginning with the development of the first phrase. So far from being diffuse or misdirected, the whole opening shows Beethoven's technique at its most magisterial, not troubling to defy conventions but treating them with Olympian disregard. Thus the detached crotchets of what ought to be the counter-subject are represented by a quite different melodic outline for the cello entry of the subject, and what would be a fourth entry in a fugue, completing the polyphony in four parts, is given with splendid effect in only two. Here the 'counter-subject' is paraphrased freely with yet another version of the crotchet figure.

With the 'second subject' the rising semitone that had largely motivated the first movement is much in evidence, combined with the rhythmic figure of the very first bar of the movement. The long dominant pedal on the second violin's open D string (note the added octave at its fifth bar) is a fine subtlety of tone-colour.

When the main quasi-fugal theme begins to develop, with very effective inversion of its first figure, the modulations lead towards

D flat as in the first movement development, but the climax, of formidable though unaggressive power, dwells on the minor of this Neapolitan key. (There is nothing enharmonic here, C sharp minor being a convenience of notation.) The most Beethovenish phrase in this splendid tirade is a conflation of elements in the two principal themes.

Ex. 41

bars 120 ff.

from bar I

from bar 64,
inverted

The metrical unit ♩ ♩♩♩ | ♩. is the one that pervades so many

works of the middle period. At some indefinable point D flat minor becomes C sharp minor, which by the semitonal change character-istic of the work (here G♯ → G♮) turns into the dominant of D minor. What follows, lightly scored and never rising above *forte*, is as compelling in power as anything in the orchestral works, simplifying the elements of music until they are abstracted into pure energy. Superficially the four eight-bar phrases repro-duce an identical scheme, but though rhythm and dynamics are unaltered and the four instruments in turn (each *sul una corda*) make an unbroken sequence out of the last figure of the main theme, the harmony is changed with an intellectual force and precision impossible to over-praise.

The rest of the development, over forty bars of sustained *fortissimo,* establishes the tonic minor, beginning with a sequence of 3 x 4 bars of dominant-seventh chords in root position pervaded by the first figure of the theme; the use of open strings here is a triumph of imaginative instrumentation. The pause in the home dominant is no mere dramatic gesture; nothing but a complete stop could stem the impetus gathered over more than sixty bars. The stroke of genius by which a new counterpoint to the theme is introduced for the recapitulation has always been admired.

At the close of the notably regular recapitulation the flourish on the home dominant returns, as at the end of the development, but there is no pause. Instead the coda begins with the prolonged trills so brilliantly exploited in the 'Waldstein' sonata. The first begins with a double augmentation of the rising semitone (two bars on F, two on F sharp) as approach to the sustained dominant, which, passed from part to part, is maintained through eighteen bars. When, after a long descent developed from the end of the theme, the first violin in its lowest register begins another *perpetuum mobile*, the material is a variation of figures from the minim counter-subject.

The Bach-like conflict between the flat and sharp leading notes is maintained to the very end and motivates the grand rhetoric of the unison *fortissimo* B flat in bar 386, a threat of the subdominant powerful enough to stop the onrush, but unable to withstand the two rising semitones of the first violin in calmly authoritative long notes (bars 389–90). Repeated by the second violin, these restore the tonic as centre for the now irresistible final climax. It is incomprehensible that modern criticism should undervalue this magnificent finale.

Op. 74 in E flat major

After completing the Rasumovsky quartets Beethoven resumed work on the C minor Symphony, and it was not until 1809 that he returned to the quartet medium with Op. 74, one of four major works in E flat written during the same period (the others being the piano sonata Op. 81a, 'Das Lebewohl', the trio Op. 70 no. 2, and the Fifth Piano Concerto).

Of all Beethoven's quartets this is perhaps the most subjective, inasmuch as its contrasts seem not altogether integrated except by reference to the composer's personality. This, it may be objected, is true of all works of art created by a major artist, but there is a sense in which the perfectly realised idea of a work liberates it from its creator, so that it becomes 'seraphically free from taint of personality'.

Thus it is possible, though not very sensible, to discuss whether the 'Eroica' is 'about' Napoleon or about Beethoven, but the symphony would remain a lucid masterpiece if nothing were known of its composer or of the First Consul.

With the 'Harp' Quartet (so called from the pizzicato figure in the first *allegro*) the situation is somewhat different. In simplified outline it consists of a *poco adagio* introduction, full of elevated sentiment like the best Schumann, a brilliantly scored quasi-symphonic *allegro*, a lyrical, richly elaborated *adagio*, a laconic scherzo alternating with a trio in deliberately rough polyphony and, for conclusion, a neatly trimmed set of variations on a good-humoured theme.

If we seek for a unifying element in this strange sequence of movements, we find only the expansion of the medium, producing not mere virtuosity but the intensification of instrumental qualities. Perhaps there is a phase in the development of certain supreme artists when the awareness of total mastery prompts a serious playing with the sheer range of expression.

Let it be granted, then, that the introduction, with its touchingly intimate subdominant opening, is too deep for what follows (is this a fault?) and would be worthy of the last quartets. (Note how it twice reaffirms the A flat side of the main key in bars 13 and 17.) In the closing bars the true subject of discourse is not the rising chromatic scale, wonderfully harmonised though it is, but the three steps of the bass on the melodic figure of the very first bar. After such a prelude the *Allegro* breaks in with blunt cheerfulness. The main subject, less simple than it appears, grandly spans a ten-bar phrase. Do not miss the counter-statement by the viola, almost hidden low down in the texture of the sustained harmonies around it. The sequel, though, is less demanding, with two chords a bar given some distinction by the pizzicato crotchets derived, without intense intellectual effort perhaps, from the first bar. When this elementary process reaches the dominant we find that Beethoven is concerned with rhythmic subtleties beyond the grasp of any listener who regards the previous eight bars as perfunctory. Their function is to spell out the simplest four-beat pattern so that it can continue as a silent background to the complexities of the rest of the transition and the second subject.

Ex. 42

bars 43 ff.

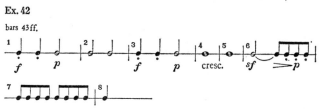

Besides the strongly characterised melodic ideas in this short exposition, the rhythmic invention is comparable with the variety of stresses within the iambic pentameter found in the blank verse of the greatest masters.

In the sketches, the abrupt change (in the final version) from B flat to the dominant of C minor at the start of the development was weakened by four explanatory bars. Ultimately the expectation of C minor is not fulfilled, being displaced by something much more impressive, with the crescendo to a grandly sustained C *major*, in which the second part of the first theme is treated with a breadth appropriate, it would seem, to a development on a scale nearer to Op. 59 no. 1 than to the present movement, with its concise exposition. In fact this is the only climax in the whole development, for with unprecedented boldness Beethoven turns everything else before the reprise into the preparation for it in a prolonged diminuendo, with mysterious tone colours found nowhere else in classical quartet style – though exploited as an effect, with less cause, later in the century. Classical ideals of proportion are treated with disrespect when Beethoven allots to the home dominant chord the last fourteen bars of this development, of which the whole span is scarcely longer than the exposition.

It is becoming clear that his concern in this movement is to contrast within a single design the most condensed and the most expansive textures. Sonata recapitulations are often shorter than expositions, but the individuality of this *Allegro* shows in a doubling of the length of the transition passage, with its pizzicato and repeated quaver chords. Everything else is closely reproduced.

By the sixteenth bar of the coda the main tonic and dominant begin to alternate in a broad rhythm suggesting that the end is not far away; but that very deliberate dominant preparation before the reprise can scarcely be left unmotivated, and a concerto-like first violin solo interrupts the expected peroration with a diminished seventh over an implied dominant pedal (bars 221 ff.). Further four-bar phrases, all on diminished sevenths, produce an unmistakable effect of preparation, but for what? The last phrase expands for two beats, and as it turns from the diminished seventh belonging to F minor to a chord in the tonic area the second violin, in canonic dialogue with the viola, brings back the grandest figure of the main theme to build a climax of symphonic power, the finest of its kind ever imagined for the string quartet and one achieved within the purest chamber music style. The closing bars, mainly on the tonic chord, are given a quieter kind of quasi-orchestral scoring disposed round the deep third of the viola. (For the orchestral equivalent see the end of the Eighth Symphony.)

Though no one but Beethoven could have written the very beautiful *Adagio*, it lacks the concentration of his finest slow movements; and the rondo-style returns of the main theme, wonderful in tone-colour, are not entirely convincing in melodic variation. Three years earlier the Fourth Symphony had shown how a lyrical melody could be enhanced by ornamentation, and soon after writing Op. 74 Beethoven began work on the B flat Trio, Op. 97, where the elementary device of varying a theme by breaking it into short notes (the *doubles* of the Baroque style) was raised to the highest level. In the quartet the decorated versions of the theme obscure its nobility of sentiment without adding any compensatory qualities. Elsewhere in the movement, notably in the D flat episode, Beethoven's 'absolute melody' prevails and the abrupt *fortissimo* before the third return of the rondo refrain (bar 110) reveals the near-tragic tension behind the luxuriance of florid decoration. By placing the *Adagio* in A flat, Beethoven relates it to the subdominant of the introduction to the first movement, and the choice of C minor and major for the scherzo banishes the earlier key with its associated sentiments; the sustained A flat chord in the transition from scherzo to finale is a further consequence of the introduction. Another example of Beethoven's large-scale tonal design in this work is the use of C, both major and minor. C major, as we have noted, is the key of the great climax in the first movement's development. It returns in alternation with C minor, in the scherzo, and the theme for the variation finale ends its first section on the dominant of C minor.

The scherzo belongs to a type intensely characteristic of Beethoven, though strangely enough of rare occurrence in his music. Between the 'Eroica' and Seventh Symphonies, a period of some eight years, there are three such pieces that spring readily to mind: in the Fifth Symphony, the A major cello sonata and this quartet. If the slow movement dwells on frustrated longing for happiness the *Presto* has something of Goethe's *Rastlose Liebe*:

> 'Dem Schnee, dem Regen,
> Dem Wind entgegen'.

It uses the 'fate-motif' of the C minor Symphony to express not only the self-conscious defiance of a few years earlier ('I will seize Fate by the throat') but the grim cheerfulness of a man who would wring the neck of that dubious personification. (See bars 43 ff. of this quartet movement, noting the second violin, then the cello.)

The trio section roars with a fierceness beyond the imagining of the actor-manager who produced the play of Pyramus and Thisbe. The pedantries of scholastic counterpoint, so amiably parodied in the 'thème russe' of Op. 59 no. 2, are here torn apart with exuberant contempt. Beethoven seems to have worked at this splendid grotesque before arriving at satisfactory material to produce the requisite 'wrongness' of which bars 106 ff. are a pleasing specimen. The second reprise of the *minore* (the movement has the scheme of the original version of the Fifth Symphony's scherzo) loses none of its force when the dynamics are scaled down as in the Fifth Symphony. The coda evidently impressed Schubert, who based on it his own *Quartettsatz* in C minor.

If the finale had used the theme originally sketched, the contrast between the *echt*-Beethoven scherzo and its sequel would have been almost cynical, for this square-cut little tune is ingratiating to excess:

Ex. 43

though it would have been at home in the Septet. Variations I–V, alternately energetic and lyrical, maintain the tonal structure of the theme in that each closes its first section on the dominant of C minor and moves to the momentary D major harmony in the twelfth bar. While variations I, III and V might be called 'studies for strings', the second and fourth reach the heights of Beethoven's incomparable lyrical inspiration. Not even Brahms glorified the viola as in II, and the violin line in IV is felicitous beyond description in its irreducible simplicity, enhanced by the change of harmonic direction where the D major chord is confidently awaited. As for the coda, the exquisite theme is treated harshly when compressed into bare octaves at the very end; but seekers after charm must look to other composers.